Ernie the Elephant

By: Leela Hope

Printed in USA

Published by: Leela Hope

In the Jungle of Nolow,
Where the wild things live,
There lived a small elephant,
With a lot of love to give.imm

Ernie was really quite big,
When he was compared to cats or dogs.
But he was small for an elephant,
He could not knock over trees or lift logs.

His father always told him,
Not to worry and to be himself,
But the other elephants teased him,
They called him shorty or Ernie the elf.

It was hard for Ernie to go to school,
There was so much teasin',
Ernie didn't know why they were so mean,
There really was no reason.

Henry was a big elephant,
And he was very popular at school,
Everyone wanted to play with him,
They all thought he was cool.

Henry did not like Ernie,
Henry told his friends,"He is too small,"
Henry decided,"If anybody plays with Ernie,
They can't be my friend at all."

The next day at recess,
Everyone went out to play,
No one would talk to Ernie,
He got so sad he ran away.

Ernie ran deep into the jungle,
His eyes were starting to tear,
He tried to get far enough away,
That nobody El could hear.

"What's wrong?" Asked a tiny voice,
Ernie looked around,
"I am down here,"
The mouse yelled from the ground.

The mouse's name was Martin,
And he knew about being small,
"And whenever you get down,"
He said, "to somebody you are tall."

"You can't let people bother you,"
Martin the mouse said,
"I know you can lift that log,
What stopped you is all in your head."

Martin jumped on Ernie head,
And they headed back to the school,
"I will be your friend," said Martin,
"Because I think you are cool."

They ran back to the school yard,
Ernie walked up to that tree,
He lifted it right over his head,
And held it up for everyone to see.

The elephants all cheered for him,
They said he was big and strong too,
"Now I am cool" said Ernie,
Cause I am just like you.

"That's not why your cool,"
Said Martin,"I am telling you,
Everyone one is cool,
When to themselves they are true."

Disclaimer - Legal Notes

Every effort has been made to accurately

represent this book and it's potential.

Results vary with every individual, and your results may or may not

be different from those depicted.

No promises, guarantees or warranties,

whether stated or implied, have been made that you

will produce any specific result from this book.

Your efforts are individual and unique,

and may vary from those shown.

Ernie Teaches Henry Not to Brag

By: Leela Hope

Ernie the elephant is not so big.

He is really rather small,

but he never gives up.

His heart is 10 feet tall!

Henry likes to tease the others.

He thinks it's lots of fun

to go around the playground shouting,

"I am better than everyone!"

The other day at school,

some kids were playing basketball.

Henry blocked a bounce pass

and played keep-away from them all.

He started to do a dance and sing,

"I am the best. I am the best, best, best!"

But the singing and dancing were too much.

He lay down and took a little rest.

The next day Henry ran the track.

He asked everyone if they wanted to be beat.

The other kids just walked away,

and Henry tripped over his own feet.

Henry was getting upset. Why were people walking away?

He needed somebody to beat, or else how could he play?

So finally he asked Ernie to race him round the track.

Henry said, "I can beat you with my trunk behind my back."

Ernie agreed to race against Henry

as long as Henry said please.

And he had to agree that

if Ernie won, Henry could no longer tease.

The race started.

Both elephants began to run.

Henry was out front.

"This is why I am number one!"

Henry continued to brag

as they circled the track.

But his pace began to slow.

Henry seemed out of whack.

Henry continued to brag

as they circled the track.

But his pace began to slow.

Henry seemed out of whack.

Ernie watched Henry waiting for the time

to pass his bragging friend.

Ernie was not tired at all.

He was saving his energy for the end.

Ernie pushed off at last.

He gave his final kick.

Henry just watched Ernie pass.

Henry was feeling sick.

Ernie won and everyone cheered.

The others were so happy.

Henry was now getting teased,

and his comebacks were not snappy.

"Stop it guys,"said Ernie.

"There is never a good reason to tease."

Henry felt terrible and he said,

"Ernie,can you forgive me, please?"

Ernie the Elephant in Martin Learns to Share

Ernie the elephant was not as big
as the other guys.
But it didn't bother him anymore;
he was okay with his size.

*Ernie's friend Martin Mouse
was way smaller than an elephant.
But his confidence made him seem
tall and strong like a giant.*

Ernie loved his little friend.
He liked to play with the mouse.
But he was always borrowing toys
When at Ernie's house.

Martin borrowed a toy train
and little soldiers, too.
Ernie did not mind the borrowing.
He said, "That's what friends do."

What bothered Ernie was the fact:
while Martin took a lot,
he never seemed to share back.
Ernie gave but never got.

So one day as they were playing,
Ernie asked his friend.
"Can I borrow your action figure?
I will bring him back this weekend."

Martin grabbed the doll
right out of Ernie's hand.
"You can't have this toy.
I need him. You understand?"

"No, I don't!" said Ernie.
The elephant was really upset.
He stood up and walked away.
His tears got the mouse all wet.

Martin felt terrible.
He had made his friend feel sad.
He didn't share his toys.
Martin knew that he had been bad.

Martin went to his mother and asked,
"Why did Ernie run away?"
His mother told him,
"Martin, you are selfish when you play."

Martin thought about all of Ernie's toys
that the mouse had asked to borrow.
Martin realized that he was not a good friend.
His heart was filled with sorrow.

Martin grabbed his favorite doll,
and he headed for Ernie's house.
"I know that I can set this right,"
he said. "I am a good little mouse."

Martin gave Ernie the toy
and said, "I didn't want you to go away."
Ernie was so happy to see his friend.
He invited the mouse in to play.

Now when Martin and Ernie play together,
Martin is always willing to share.
The little mouse has learned that
sharing tells friends you care.

Ernie the Elephant and the Teddy Bear

By Leela Hope

Printed in USA

Published by: Leela Hope

© Copyright 2017

ISBN-10:

ISBN-13:

Ernie was an elephant,

though not as big as some.

He wasn't scared of the dark

as long as he had Plum.

Plum's a purple teddy bear

that Ernie's had for a while.

The little toy helps him sleep

and has always made him smile.

Then, just after suppertime,

before he went to bed,

Plum was nowhere to be seen –

Ernie was filled with dread.

He ran into the laundry,

"Maybe he's lost in there."

He searched through the laundry pile –

where is his little bear?

Next, he searched the living room –

the couch and coffee table.

He wished he could find his bear –

He did all he was able.

Martin Mouse was Ernie's friend

and he wanted to help.

"What we have's a mystery,"

said Martin, "please, don't yelp."

"We need to ask some questions,"

he said and tweaked his whiskers.

"Your parents might know something,"

said Martin in hushed whispers.

"Where did you hide the bear?"

Martin yelled at Ernie's dad.

He just glared at Martin

and said, "Yelling makes me mad!"

So, they quickly went on their way

and soon found Ernie's Mom.

She said, "You should retrace your steps

from where you started from."

Ernie said, "I had Plum in bed,

but what did I do then?

Maybe he is in the bathroom –

I brushed my teeth again."

So, they checked the bathroom,

but his bear they could not see.

"I think I got dressed next –

Maybe that is where he'd be."

Ernie dove through all the clothes

and Martin searched around.

But when they both reappeared,

Plum still remained unfound.

"Then I got a glass of milk!"

Ernie said when he recalled.

The friends took off like lightning –

they raced right down the hall.

The bear was in the kitchen!

And leaning on the bread.

Ernie gave that bear a hug

and took him back to bed.

About the Author

Leela Hope is a writer with over 22 years of experience

in writing endearing children's fiction.

Her lively characters have entranced and

captivated her audience, and she has taken

great joy in writing the three series of books,

each beautifully illustrated with love and care.

Her stories concentrate on the adventures of floppy eared

bunnies and wide-eyed children learning lessons in life,

before returning home wiser and eager for sleep.

leela hope writes her stories to entertain the v

ery young, but also to educate.

Her vision is always of a parent sitting on a

child's bed, reciting

the stories each night,

while the young one drifts off to sleep,

lulled into a dream world full of fun and adventure.

From her very earliest years of childhood,

leela made up stories in her head, telling them to her younger brother and sister.

The stories flowed easily from her mind,

and it wasn't long before she realized she had

a gift for writing. By the age of 14, she had already written a small

book of short stories for her own entertainment,

and by the age of 22, she had published her first

full-fledged children's fiction in several magazines

leela hope was destined to be an author and she

knew exactly what genre of fiction she wanted to dedicate her life too.

Born in San Diego, California, and still residing in the area,

leela studied English Literature at Berkeley, earning a degree in 1989.

Her writing covers a span of several genres,

but she always returns to her first love,

children's fiction. She enjoys scuba diving and visiting wildlife parks,

seeking new inspiration for cuddly characters for her stories.

leela hope lives in an urban area of San Diego and is presently at work on a new book.

http://www.leelahope.net/

Disclaimer - Legal Notes

Every effort has been made to accurately

represent this book and it's potential.

Results vary with every individual, and your results may or may not

be different from those depicted.

No promises, guarantees or warranties,

whether stated or implied, have been made that you

will produce any specific result from this book.